Freed to flourish

Melody Ayers

Presentation by *BookLeaf Publishing*

Web: www.bookleafpub.com

E-mail: info@bookleafpub.com

ISBN: 9789358314472

First edition 2023

Suffering Psalm

There was no warning
No gentle easing into the water
A clay vessels shattered
By the hands of the potter
My peaceful river
Now a raging sea
All your waves and breakers
Crashing over me
My tree of hope
Torn up by its roots
The rising water
Destroyed its fruits
The clouds grow darker
A storm stirs in the east
The waves are rising
Like a ravenous beast
In a broken ship
I'm sent out to sea
The roaring winds
Cry out, no mercy, no mercy
I cannot see the shore
The lighthouse it grows dim
The monsters of the deep
They know I cannot swim
I'm forced to dwell in darkness

With no one to deliver
The Lord has bent his bow
And is emptying his quiver
Have you wrapped yourself in clouds
So no prayer can pass through?
Have you wrapped yourself in anger?
My pain you will pursue
Is there a whisper in the wind
A whisper of some hope
A clearing in the mist
A singing phalarope
The morning always comes
His mercy never ceases

Once I'm broken on the rock
Will he put back all the pieces?
But for now I'm sinking fast
The waves begin to rise
The glimmer of some light
Was only the moonrise
Come in the moon
Come in the seas
Bring mercy in the moonrise
As the waves crash over me

Collide

3

The sea can be peaceful or terrifying,
Both can be beautiful if I am safe on shore

This is my heart

Frozen in winter
The icicles grow
Deadly, alluring
like rhythms from Poe
Poison and venom
from the deadliest creature
Words dripped in seduction
make the most cunning preacher
Consumed in a wasteland
my heart made of stone
Crushed in the teeth
of a jackal's jaw bone
My road is despair
its path leads to death
The roads winding wide
dismay is its breath
Black is my color
In darkness I dwell
I've never seen light
but the fires of hell
My companions are nightmares
dragons of the abyss
The devil my master
and anguish my bliss
I need my heart broken

I know I must die
Desires need woken
to shred me inside
Whatever it takes
my heart life or soul
All I hold dear
then let it be so
Don't give me tomorrow
I need to feel shame
Your voice should bring fear
the reproach from your name
Can my stone turn to flesh?
is there hope for my heart?
Can you bring life to bones?
Can you paint a new art?
I'm filthy in rags
I despise who I've been
An abscessed infection
I disgust at my sin
I see blood, pain and weeping
it should be my own
I see a man dying
the Sine qua non
The ice starts to melt

Meditation

I made a circle of flowers
and then I went and sat inside
I closed my eyes and tried to feel
all the things I try to hide

Body Speaks

Something is wrong
My body screamed
Pain, disfunction silencing my song
Stop! Listen!
Something is not right
Why can't you see?
Stuck in fight or flight
Unacknowledged anger
makes my body shake
Unprocessed pain
makes my body ache

Him

Alcohol is favorite mistress
He drinks and she tells him drink more
Porn is his favorite mistress
Abuse she says is what woman adore
I was his favorite mistress
Sex, cook, bear children, do all his chores
I was the wife he abandoned
when I couldn't take anymore

Mystification

Call me Mara
my life is bitter
A large infection has come
from a small splinter
I went away full
I came back empty
I was given gifts
stores of plenty
God gave, God takes away
Yet I'm supposed to say
blessed be your name?
I will argue my way to your face
Your supposed to be good
How is this grace?

Others opinion of my grief

What is grief?
I don't want to feel this pain
They say, "I have to feel this pain."
It will bring relief
How long will it last?
I don't want to feel this pain
They say, "embrace the pain"
Dig into your past
How will I survive if I feel all this pain?
I'm going insane
I was meant to thrive
They say, "there is no way out but through it."
I don't want to feel this pain
They say,
"Just embrace it and pursue it"
"But also smile"
"Pretend you don't feel pain"
"You should see past the pain"
"It should only last a little while"
"You should sing through the trial"
"Embrace the growth from pain"
"Don't forget to smile"

Shipwreck

We were on a ship
On the sea
A raging storm

I could see the land before this black
We once hoped to thrive
Now I just hope to survive
You steered us into the storm
You want us to drown?

Stop thrashing
Calm down
Or we're going to drown

I found a piece of driftwood
You crashed the ship up on the rocks
Your trying to hold my driftwood
Why?
You crashed the ship?

I can see the sword again
A beautiful island
But I can't make it to shore with you on my
driftwood
Do I push you off?

Do I let you drown?
Do I drift forever?
I love you
You sunk the ship!

Strength

Standing at the base of a mountain
It's beauty is in its strength
If no one will love you, love yourself
Standing at the shore of the ocean
It's waters can wash away pain
The spray of the foam is refreshing
It holds secrets only God knows
It's beauty is in its strength
If the whole world loves you, still love yourself
Standing at the mountain
The way is hard, the trail is long
But at the summit the view was worth the climb
The beauty of the mountain is its strength
Love yourself
The beauty of the mountain is its power
Love yourself
The woods are thick, the way is dark
But the smell of the pine is refreshing
The sun is leaking through the trees
dancing through the branches
bringing light to the path
The beauty of the forest is its strength
The secrets, the mysteries that want to be seen
Begging for light
Begging for a summit view

For the tide to return to the sea
So I can see what is beneath my feet
What is true?
The fog is lifting
The sun is rising
The beauty of a woman is her strength

Body Memories

Hands hold memories
His hand in mine
His fingers playing a song on the imaginary
piano of my hand
I loved that!
Feet hold memories
His hands massaging my feet
My feet ache and king for his touch now
The memories of his abuse are taking over
I'm surrounded by walls of memories
I see a picture and I remember how unkind he
was
How hard I had to fight for that smile
I remember him acting like he didn't remember
we planned family pictures
I remember the trigger
My body knows something is wrong
But he promised everything was okay
It turned out my body was right
He was drunk for that picture
He didn't come home that night
In my children's eyes I see three birthday he
ruined
He stole that day from her and I
I start to wonder why I miss him

Why I love him
My body is terrified of him
My body remembers
But also,
Deep down inside my body remembers that it
loves him
Even if it can't remember why

Fight

I love you
But there is a monster inside me
It's taking me over
When I need to be seen
When I need to feel safe
Rage is how I hide
Who I am
Th vulnerable parts of me

Flight

Eye on the exit
I'm facing the door
Stop it! Just stop it!
I can't can't anymore
How do I rest
when I always have to run?
I must do my best
Everything must be done
If I get it all right
Maybe you'll love me
Stuck in this flight
Flying to break free

Freeze

Sometimes my body holds me captive against
my will
Frozen, forcing quiet, solitude
Be still
Listen!
What is she trying to say?
Thank her
Honor her
That spirit inside you
Was put there to guide you

Fawn

I'm a mimick
I'm a mine
An empty shell
I'm always fine
Absorbed into you
I disappear
Alive, present
But not really here
Defending bad behavior
Because trauma is a monster
And my cage feels safer

The Painting

I wish I could paint a picture, then I would paint
a picture of you
A man, filthy and disgusting that the artist is
making new
I would make my painting large
A master piece of art
I would put in a museum and pray with all my
heart one day you would walk by and see what I
could do
You would stop and study the painting and see
that it was you
You would see sadness inside one eye and hope
inside the other
You would see beauty calling out, begging you
to discover that even monsters can be redeemed
Even captives can be freed
And the longer you stop and stare the more
beauty and hope is there
I hope I'm at the museum that day and you turn
around and see me
For the first time you really see me because you
see that I've always seen you

Fall's end

Yellow, red, orange, vibrant
Leaves that were beautiful are now falling fast
Brown, beige, full, one demensional
A reminder the beauty was not meant to last

Seasonal depression

I dreaded the coming of fall
The cold, the rain, the wind
But the colors this year are fire
Reminding me every season holds beauty
I smile, my voice gasps out loud
Beauty surrounds me
I love it
Stay autumn, stay
Hold off the coming of winter
The cold, the snow, the wind
But maybe this year my eyes have been opened
to its beauty
The snow will be pure
I will smile, gasp out loud
Beauty will surround me
I will love it
Stay winter, stay
Hold off the coming of spring

Morning light

The sun is slowly making an appearance
I can't see it, but I can see the signs
There is a mysterious grey light giving definition
to the trees
A mist
The birds are waking up with song
Just like that there is light
No sound, no dance, just sudden light
I can see again
The morning came

Song birds

25

It's early morning
Tit mice dance in the wind
bobbing up and down
braving my presence for food
Chickadees singing their favorite song
Are you here God?
Do you hear me?
What are you doing?
The birds start to fly wildly
Their songs get louder
God is reminding me
He cares for sparrows
He will take care of me
Even the frightened song of the birds holds
beauty

Hope Note

Remember the mountain. You couldn't see it
yesterday. It was hiding in the fog
The sun wasn't shining.
Today the sun is shining. Today you can see the
mountain.
Remember the mountain of God.
I am always there. I am always with you.
Even to the ends of the earth.
Even when the fog is thick and you cannot see
me and the sun isn't shining.
I'm still here, just like that mountain.
When the days vanish like smoke. When the
grass withers and is blighted. When you forget
to eat. When you lay awake groaning. When
your enemies tail against you and make you eat
ash, I will turn your ash into beauty.
I sit enthroned on high.
I am the God who saved you from the mouth of
the lion, from the paw of the bear, and I will
deliver you from this.
They may come against you with sword, spear
and javelin.
But I AM the living God.
I AM your God, the God of armies.
When you call I will answer.

I will deliver those who have defiled.
I will deliver them into your hands.
They will say, "There is a God in heaven."
"The Lord saves."
When you are a bird alone sitting on the rooftop,
singing your lament.
When your drink is tears, say to your soul,
"Soul, why are you downcast? Hope in God."
I will come sit beside you on that rooftop.
I will collect all your tears in my bottle.
I will add my tears. I will add my blood.
I will sing your lament with you, and then I will
give you a new song.
For I will do marvelous things.
I love you.
I have called you by name.
You will clap your hands.
You are mine.

www.ingramcontent.com/pod-product-compliance
Lightning Source LLC
LaVergne TN
LVHW021358200726

843509LV00014B/2922